# Princess Diana

## The True Story of the People's Princess

Katy Holborn

The People's Princess…this is her story.

# 'It was a bit crowded...'

When Diana entered St Paul's cathedral, chosen ahead of royalty's normal wedding venue Westminster Abbey, because of its extra capacity, she seemed to have everything.

Beauty, a sense of style and occasion, the hand of the future king, the adoration of a public overwhelmed with affection for her.

Six hundred thousand people lined the streets to cheer her on the way to Cathedral, with a further 750 million worldwide glued to their TV sets.

Her wedding dress, train trailing 25 feet behind her, cost £9000 and accentuated every aspect of her physical charms and engaging character.

But as early as the service itself came a hint that this was not a woman who would quietly assume the role of a subordinate in her relationship with Charles.

Saying his name the wrong way round – she said Philip Charles – was a genuine error, but the couple's decision to omit the word 'obey' from their marriage vows raised more than the odd eyebrow.

Although it is often missed out these days, couples feeling, quite reasonably, that any relationship based on obedience has no place in modern Western society, this was not the case in the early '80s.

And particularly when the marriage was a royal occasion. The monarchy, an institution steeped in tradition, duty, and protocol, was not (at least then) a place in which change was embraced.

New ideas, new ways of bringing up a family, new opinions on the natural hierarchy – these had to be chewed over, endlessly reviewed, before they could be implemented.

In her quiet, understated but thoroughly determined manner, Diana did not work that way.

Diana Spencer met Prince Charles in 1977. At the time, there was much speculation around the love life of the future monarch, and he was dating Diana' sister, Sarah (later Lady Sarah McQuorquodale).

The story goes that Diana was somewhat in awe of the heir to the throne at the time.

Beyond that, the occasion was not noteworthy.

The first indication that love was on the horizon came three years later.

Charles and Diana had both, separately, been invited to a country weekend. On that fateful summer's day, Charles was involved in a polo match and Diana watched him play.

They spoke, and a spark was ignited.

He then invited her to a sailing weekend at Cowes, aboard the royal yacht. Following the short stay on Brittanica, he took her to 'meet the family'.

The royals were staying in their Scottish home, Balmoral, and both the Queen and her husband were taken with the stunning young lady, not yet out of her teens.

Dates followed in London and in February 1981, with rumors growing about their relationship, Prince Charles asked Diana to marry him. She was deeply in love and accepted.

Her engagement ring cost £30000 and consisted of 14 diamonds in a white gold setting. A blue Ceylon Sapphire completed the design. The Queen Mother gave her a diamond and sapphire broach to compliment her choice.

Could life get any better for a young girl?

In the press conference following their announcement, they were asked if they are marrying for love.

An odd choice of question to bring up, perhaps, but stories had circulated about a relationship in the background involving Charles and a married woman, Camilla Parker-Bowles.

They had known each other for years, but Camilla had married, and so any relationship beyond friendship was, for a royal, out of the question.

Watching the interview with Charles and Diana now, we can understand their responses in the context of what happened since. At the time, Diana appears bemused by being asked whether they were marrying for love.

Why else would they be?

'Of course,' she answers and offers that gentle smile which was already winner hearts around the world.

Her consort, though, adds, (mysteriously and not without a little apparent discomfort): 'Whatever love means'

Five months of intense interest and news coverage later, the big day arrived.

Many years later, following separation and divorce, Diana allowed journalist Martin Bashir to hold what became a seminal interview with her.

Broadcast on the BBC's flagship documentary show Panorama, the journalist asks her about the marriage.

Her response is telling. 'Well, there were three of us in this marriage, so it was a bit crowded.' If the words are ironic, then her face and tone of voice suggest a deep sadness and regret about how things turned out.

Even before wedlock took place, early signs of rifts were beginning to emerge. Diana discovered a bracelet with the initials G and F inscribed on it.

Camilla and Charles called themselves Gladys and Fred. It was one of the Charles' 'Goon Show' inspired jokes.

Such was his fiance's anxiety about the wedding that she wrote to a friend stating that 'she' (widely assumed to be Camilla) was always around.

The wife to be felt threatened, and suggested that a planned holiday to Australia should be postponed. She felt that it would be unwise for her to be so far away at this time.

In the end, Diana went on the trip, but the pressures led to the first manifestations of the future princess's eating disorder, bulimia.

Charles, too, had doubts. Perhaps the gorgeous country girl was more complex than he had thought? Perhaps his own upbringing had not taught him to deal with women like Diana.

Whatever, he is alleged to have cried 'I can't go through with it,' on the eve of the ceremony.

Charles is said to have taken a photograph of Camilla on the honeymoon, and the third person was an ever-present cloud over their relationship.

The Prince and Princess began to grow apart very quickly. Diana was interested in fashion, style, and everyday subjects. Charles favored history and architecture. There was little in common.

Maybe the question about marrying for love was not as strange as it first appeared.

Circumstances partly changed with the birth of William, their first child. The pregnancy had been difficult for Diana, with much sickness.

There were days when she was so ill that she could not get out of her bed. Charles found it all hard to cope with. His upbringing had involved much more 'manning up' and his, at times, fragile wife perplexed him.

The couple were living between Kensington Palace, their London home, and Highgrove House, their country retreat.

However, whilst staying in Sandringham, Diana had a bad fall.

Although she suffered bad bruising, their child was unhurt. Sympathy and understanding came from the Queen – she reduced Diana's official engagements – but Charles found it harder to cope.

Having been brought up very much in the style of 'Get on with it' he could not understand the issues his wife was facing.

The endless curiosity and fascination about her pregnancy contributed to her state of health.

'I believe that the whole of England lay with me during labor,' she said later.

Whilst such support and interest was given with the best of intentions, it laid enormous pressure on the young mother.

But, despite the turmoil, the pregnancy progressed and soon a new second in line to the throne arrived.

Charles was besotted with his young son. Born on 21st June 1982, Prince William was a healthy, bouncing, baby.

Royal responsibilities and photographs over, the couple retired in private for a short time.

Charles bought his wife a diamond necklace to express his delight.

But post-natal depression followed, and – as can afflict any mother – Diana fell into a pit of angst. Another downturn on their rollercoaster marriage.

Once it passed, there seems to have been a period of happiness for the family of three. With both parents captivated by their son, finally, there was something in common for them to share.

But royal duty and commitment gave little if any thought to family matters.

When he was just nine months old, a state visit to Australia threatened to separate the mother and child. Diana refused to go without her son and a stand-off ensued.

The Palace believed that the child was too young to travel such a distance, and should stay in England to be looked after by a nanny.

After all, that was what would have happened with the Queen's own children.

Swords were drawn, stances taken… and Diana won. Another indication that royal traditions would have to change.

The tour was a huge success with crowds enthralled by the royal visit.

Diana became pregnant for the second time, and this time Charles prepared thoroughly for the pregnancy, learning all he could about potential problems.

When Harry was born on 15th September 1984, both parents were once again delighted.

But tensions began to emerge all too quickly. Diana threw herself fully into parenthood, playing silly games with her children, roller skating along the corridors of Kensington Palace.

Whilst Nannies had played major roles in the lives of her husband and mother in law, Diana could become jealous of their relationship with her sons, and – perhaps understandably – made sure that they played a minor role in family life.

Whilst Charles could see the fun that they were having, his background meant that he always had an eye on his sons' future responsibilities. Even when they were of pre-school age.

Discipline, manners, sensible behavior – not always the most immediate characteristics of young children – needed to be imbued as soon as possible.

Charles wished to follow royal tradition when it came to education – a private tutor for the early years before a boarding Prep school. By contrast, Diana was of the opinion that the boys should mix with children of their own age.

With the Queen supporting her son's views, Diana was under pressure to conform but believed that her sons should grow up as normally as possible. Her views prevailed.

Soon after Harry was born, it was apparent to those close to the couple that their marriage was descending towards complete breakdown.

Diana developed a relationship with a soldier, Major James Hewitt. Their alliance would last for five years.

At the same time, she was aware that Charles and Camilla were having an affair.

Although she raised this with both her husband and, later, the Queen, with neither did she receive any assurances, nor indeed any opportunity to express her own feelings.

The matter was not one for discussion.

Like so many others, it was a marriage cracking up, with two young sons innocently caught at the center.

She considered taking the children to Australia but knew that such a move would be prohibited.

It would also appear that she was running away from her own problems. During the years in the late 1980s, her eating disorder became worse, and she attempted suicide on more than one occasion.

She even feared that members of the royal establishment would try to have her sectioned for mental illness.

Whilst the marriage had little hope for success from the outset, Diana was not completely innocent in its break up.

As well as her affair with James Hewitt, she is said to have had brief relationships with two other men whilst still married.

However, for a young and inexperienced girl to be thrust into a world where every move is analyzed by the media, where her husband has another love and where tradition and protocol overrule compassion and family, she deserves great sympathy.

Diana sought to ensure that her side of the story was publicized. In a series of interviews, she told her tale, often via a confidant, to journalist Andrew Motion.

Clearly a woman in deep distress, she poured out the truths of ten years of unhappy marriage.

Whilst rumors abounded about the state of their relationship, no formal announcement had been made regarding its future when Motion's subsequent book was serialized from June 1992.

The reaction of the establishment to Diana's story was extreme. An MP (misreading public opinion – Diana remained extremely popular) said that the author should be imprisoned in the Tower.

The book was condemned by the Archbishop of Canterbury and banned from some bookshops. The Establishment reacts badly to any threats to its status.

Diana was apparently terrified of the consequences that might follow. Exposing the truth about anything connected with the royal family was, in those times, considered traitorous.

And if that no longer meant a trip to the Tower, it could still see a person ruined, their reputation savaged, like a dog's toy, and destroyed.

All news had to be carefully spun, sanitized and approved. All comments carefully considered.

But, having endured an insufferable ten years marked by loneliness and an 'uncaring' husband, she told her story.

And never uttered a word of regret.

On December 9th of that year, it was officially announced that the couple had separated. Just under four years later, on August 28th, 1996, they divorced.

As with any break up, there were faults on both sides. A large difference in age and the initial pressure on Charles to marry may also have played their part.

And, perhaps, a clash of cultures occurred. Diana came from a wealthy, aristocratic background, but growing up away from the glare of publicity she had matured into a modern woman.

She wanted things for herself and her children to be as normal as possible. Although she recognized that there would constant media interest, she did not anticipate the extent of this.

And although she realized that the royal family is more than a family, but an institution with all the trappings that comes with this, she did not understand the scale of the pressure to conform.

The monarchy learned from the experience and does deserve credit for doing so, but it is sad that this came too late to save the 'marriage made in heaven'.

# Growing Up

It was not exactly a normal childhood, but then much of Diana's early years were spent living just a mile away from the Queen's home at Sandringham, and there was fun to be had.

Park House was a part of the Royal estate, and the younger princes, Andrew and Edward, would frequently visit to play in the Spencer's pool when they were staying in the Norfolk home.

A favorite past time of the young Diana would be to slide down the long wooden banister of the main staircase.

Climbing trees and locking unsuspecting nannies in the loo formed a part of the mischievous girl's early years.

In those days, many hours were spent playing with and looking after her younger brother, Charles.

Diana was a very caring sister – certainly, she had a naughty streak – but she protected her brother, particularly through the tricky times that were to hit the family not far into the future.

It is easy to see how these early years were the blueprint for the enormously popular and loved figure she was to become.

The combination of natural compassion mixed with the mystery of living in a world about which most of us can only dream were a perfect recipe for public adulation. But that was still to come.

Her first school, Silfield, was in nearby Kings Lynn.  Like many small independent schools, it later closed, there being just too little demand in the under populated area.

As with much of the aristocracy in those days, she was also home educated for a spell.

Big school started when she moved to a boarding Prep in Diss.  Riddlesworth Hall is still going strong and boasts a delightful portrait of the adult Diana.

The school is housed in a magnificent building, with acres of fields, and Diana would have enjoyed the freedom of playing in the grounds.

It's easy to see how she would later want a similar sort of experience for her own sons.

Her final years at school, in England at least, were further away from home. West Heath Girls' School (like Silfield, no longer operating – although it is now a special school) was based in Sevenoaks, Kent.

Academia did not fall naturally to the future Princess. Her passions were for sport and dancing. She was talented at both.

Whilst at Prep School, she showed her prowess in the pool – perhaps all those days playing with the young Princes Edward and Andrew paid dividends.

She won countless awards and trophies. She kept swimming for leisure and fitness right through her life.

She also became a talented skier and tennis player. However, in perhaps an early indication that enthusiasms between her and the royals would not be shared, horses held little interest for her.

Little girls and ponies are normally a perfect marriage, but Diana was not a girly girl, more of a tom boy. She also fell off a horse at an early age, and her interest stopped there.

Perfect marriages seemed destined to elude her.

But if sport was a passion, her true love was dancing. She retained her fascination for ballet throughout her marriage to Charles. He, of course, preferred opera.

It was her life's ambition to become a ballerina, but she grew too tall. This is yet another piece in the jigsaw of awe she created in the public.

We can all understand dreams – and when somebody as privileged as a princess has a dream which, like many of ours, fails to come to fruition, a link is forged.

The non academic aspects of school were those she most enjoyed. On top of her sport and dancing, she won an 'Helpfulness' award at Riddlesworth Hall, and her caring and considerate nature was frequently mentioned.

But we mostly attend school for the exam results we achieve. Whilst Diana's background was easily wealthy enough for her not to need qualifications, she failed to pass any O levels.

She left West Heath at 16, and – as was the case for many of her ilk in those days – went on to finishing school in Switzerland.

These kinds of institutions exist to help girls learn the rules and protocols of the society in which they will mix. This was not for Diana, and she left before her courses were complete.

Her father, Johnnie Spencer, had been a royal equerry to both the young Queen Elizabeth and her father, King George. Her grandmother had been a lady in waiting to the Queen mother.

Her family was steeped in royal tradition, but Diana seemed to challenge this all the way.

Maybe this was because she was, like most teenagers, rebellious towards her family. Or perhaps the life-changing event that took place when she was just six played its part.

Diana was still a tiny girl when her parents split up. 'It was devastating' she later said.

A world that had seemed ideal; gorgeous house, siblings and royal friends with whom to play, suddenly destroyed.

Certainly, her parents' marriage had been rocky for some years. However, to what extent this is understood by a six year old is something about which we can only speculate.

All the evidence points to a little girl who had the most wonderful early years of life. Then everything fell apart.

'I can still hear the crunch of the gravel as she walked down the drive,' she said of her mother's departure; the impact on the young Diana was life-changing.

One of her nannies, Mary Clark, told of her first meeting with the youngster. Clark describes her as 'the girl with the downcast eyes'. Diana was just nine at the time.

The Spencer children were used as pawns in a bitter divorce. Eventually, and unusually - especially for the time, custody was awarded to her father.

Diana's mother, Frances, had fallen in love with an Australian wallpaper magnate, Peter Shand Kydd.

It is also thought that the large age gap between her and her Diana's father had contributed to the break up.

She was just eighteen when she had been married, with the Queen as a guest, in Westminster Abbey.

This difference in age would, of course, be echoed when Diana married Charles years later.

Her mother left the family home and lived between London, Scotland and a farm in New South Wales, Australia.

Her own marriage to Shand Kydd ended in 1988.

The Park House home was rented and not the true home of the Spencer clan. This was Althorp, a magnificent stately home in Northamptonshire.

The house had been purchased by the Spencer family in 1508, for the princely sum of £800. It remains the seat of the family to this day.

The current Earl, the 9th, is Charles Spencer. The same Charles who played with his sister Diana those long years ago in a house on the Queen's estate in Sandringham.

The upkeep of such a home is frighteningly expensive. There remain doubts that the House can remain in the family for many more generations.

Large quantities of furnishings and paintings have periodically been auctioned off. In the early 90s, the house was losing approaching half a million pounds a year.

Although it is open to the public, that income is insufficient to keep it running. A major clear out in 2010, if such a phrase can be used to describe the quality of the goods auctioned, raised £21 million.

Quite a car boot sale!

However, half of that was required to refurbish the roof.

In 1976, Diana's grandfather died, and her father became the 8th Earl Spencer. The home in Sandringham was vacated and the family moved to Althorp.

As magnificent as Park House had been, it was very different to the sprawling, slightly austere, edifice into which Diana now moved.

By this stage, she was well into her schooling at West Heath, so time spent in the country seat was limited to school holidays.

But if Diana's passion for sport and dance remained, a new love had entered her life.

Probably caused by a reaction to her own parents' acrimonious divorce, Diana had developed a fixation with finding true love, followed by marriage and a large family.

She had said to her nanny: 'I will never marry unless I'm really in love because if you're not in love you'll get divorced.

'I'm never going to get divorced.' Profound words indeed from a young girl. Mary Clark, the nanny, went on to say that Diana's dream became to find true love, be happily married and have children.

A hope that exists in the hearts and minds of young girls throughout the land.

The irony of that wish is hard to bear, given the circumstances that would follow when she was just a few years older.

And the irony is doubled, tripled when we know that Diana had an object upon which to direct that young love.

The girl who had played in her swimming pool with the young princes had, from the age of twelve, dreamt of marrying their brother, Prince Charles.

But this ambition would not bear fruit just yet.

Ending her stay at Institut Alpin Videmanette, the Swiss finishing school, after just a term, Diana returned to England, staying at her mother's London flat with friends.

Like many school leavers as yet uncertain what to do with their lives, she bounced from job to job.  Pre school play leader, nanny, babysitting, even cleaning for a bit.

She eventually found work as an assistant at the Young England nursery school in Knightsbridge.

On turning eighteen, her mother bought a London flat for her as a present.  She moved there, again sharing with mates.

It was during this period that her friendship began to develop with Charles.

As rumors grew and press interest mounted, it became hard to even get to her work through the streams of photographers hounding her.

Just prior to the announcement of her engagement, she left her post to prepare for her wedding.

The dream she had held since early childhood, that had morphed into a fascination for one particular man, was about to become true.

# A Different Kind of Royal Mother

It's an interesting place, Eton. For a start, there is only one way in. Just off the main Windsor to Slough dual carriageway, fractionally south of the M4, is the turning.

You follow a road round a long, sweeping bend, cross a roundabout, listen and watch the low flying Jumbos, wheels already down, heading for nearby Heathrow, and enter the town.

The only other access is across the Thames, via a humped bridge that connects to Windsor and the railway station, but this bridge is usually closed to traffic.

Enormous swathes of playing fields pass by on your left, and ahead the harsh stone of the Eton Chapel dominates.

This edifice, a beacon for tourists out of term time, stretches to the classroom in which the Headmaster has sole use for teaching, his desk raised on a dais.

Seeing the room, it is like retreating to Victorian England.

The Chapel itself is cold and austere. The high backed pews face each other and the acoustics are terrible.

Built in days gone by, when humans were generally smaller, the pews are separated into individual seats by protruding narrow wooden beams.

These are too small for anybody bigger than the average twelve years old.

The result is an uncomfortable experience. Whether sermons nullify the discomfort is hard to tell. Whatever, it makes a man of you.

The top end of the town is given over to the trappings of Eton College. Enormous boarding houses are everywhere, and teaching blocks look like red brick houses.

Fives Courts and real tennis compete with a modern gymnasium and swimming pool.

Fives is everything you would associate with British aristocratic values. A game full of terms such as blackguard and pepperpot, where any contention results in a sharp call of 'Let!'

Originating from the only space the boys could play ball, a section of the Eton Chapel wall (you can still make it out) the court is full of ledges, steps, and buttresses.

Visit the town during an early Summer evening and, other than the number of teenage boys wandering around, nothing seems too unusual.

But spotted amongst the young men will be seen some who are still in their uniform. Winged collar, stud, tailcoat and dark grey bags.

Further along, the High Street comes the town proper, with banks and newsagents, but every other shop is still designed to serve the College or the tourism it generates.

Uniform shops, replica scarves (oddly vying with American baseball caps in touristy windows) surround you. This is the world into which the two princes were pushed.

A world that appears isolated and unreal, where the beaks (teachers) are still provided with waitress service at lunch and almost all are housed within the school's properties.

But in reality, whilst still a bastion of privilege, Eton tries to play its part in a more modern world. It recently opened a nearby Free School, so that those less wealthy could experience Eton like learning.

It provides substantial bursaries to those whom it feels would benefit from an Eton Education.

Awards are intensely competitive, but the school will, for some, provide free teaching, uniform, food, trips and accommodation.

The young princes' father and grandfather had been sent far away, to Gordonstoun in northern Scotland, for their secondary education, but Diana was determined to break with this tradition.

Although not the kind of school everybody can (or would even choose to) attend, it was close to home and the cultural mix of pupils was good.

The press still delights in presenting Eton College as a last stand of the empire, a home to privilege and opportunity and to some extent it is.

But it also has, for a school of its kind, a broad and diverse intake of children.

Football (which the boys loved) is its main sport. It offers a wide curriculum and, although full boarding forms a compulsory element of the children's lives, is open to parental visits.

The Princes' first school had been a small London pre Preparatory establishment – again a break with tradition as royals had usually been educated at home.

But Diana had insisted that they should get an insight into how the real world operates.

Cheam School, near Newbury, had been their father and grandfather' prep (for children aged 8-13) but the Princess wanted her children closer to home.

She chose, against opposition from the royal family, Ludgrove School near Wokingham.

This, she felt, would provide a more normal education and also the security the Princes would need – both from the press and more sinister operators.

Charles and she had reached a deal with the media. In return for occasional stories and updates, the boys would be left alone.

Ludgrove is an interesting choice. It does not have the grand buildings of many other private schools.

It is almost unnoticed from the road. From a highly ordinary housing estate on the outskirts of Wokingham, a drive past a level crossing leads to a gate on your right.

Pig pens, ponds and fields greet you left and right, and you have no sense of having entered a school as you drive endlessly down what seems to be a paved farm track.

Finally, on the left, are some fairly unattractive modern houses.

These were in fact built to house the security staff who would be ever present whilst the princes were at the school.

At last, the entrance is on your left, and pulls into a small circular drive fronting what looks like a slightly larger than the average house, but is, in fact, the school.

One of the main attractions of Ludgrove is its closeness to London. The school sits amongst a hive of similar schools just outside the M25.

Sport takes center stage in places such as these, and every Wednesday and Saturday would be fixtures, which Diana would attend whenever possible.

Teachers report of her sitting under a tree, watching her boys play cricket, football or rugby. A quiet figure, with a generous smile and approachable nature.

Not really very different from the other parents.

Of the boys' father, the staff can report no sightings.

With her marriage falling apart, her sons became the focal point of her life. William, the elder, her confidant – the man of the family.

And Harry, the younger, her little boy, to cuddle and protect. This treatment became reflected in their behavior. William was regarded as mostly sensible, reliable and mature.

His brother was the rascal, getting into trouble and scrapes throughout much of his school career.

We can only draw judgments from the evidence we have because the royal family was (and still is to a lesser extent) a secretive institution.

But Charles had grown up with, whilst undoubtedly loving parents, a mother, and father who saw their duties to the nation and Commonwealth as paramount.

For Diana, her *children* were paramount. Because of the mutually agreed media embargo, little is known about the Princes' school days.

But snippets from teachers who taught them tell of two remarkably normal boys.

Mostly good but occasionally troublesome; stories of riding in the back of a teacher's car with other friends, the security cars following behind.

Polite, well brought up boys. Privileged, but in many ways very normal.

Except of course, from the ages of 15 and 12, they grew up without a mum.

The image of the boys walking behind her coffin at her funeral is one that is seared into the national consciousness

Along with Prince Charles, Prince Philip and Diana's brother Charles Spencer, they stepped out in front of the hundreds of thousands lining the streets to Westminster Abbey.

Harry had been uncertain what to do. His Grandfather said to him 'If I walk, will you come with me?' The boys' bouquet on top of the coffin said simply 'Mummy'.

To lose a parent is always deeply upsetting. To do so in avoidable circumstances adds to the misery.

To be just a child when it happens is almost impossible to perceive, but to have that event shared by the entire nation is beyond our comprehension.

The boys had been in Sandringham when the news of Diana's death had broken and were protected from some of the national outpouring by the Queen and Philip.

The royals bore the brunt of media and public anger about this decision, but it was right and put the interests of the boys first.

As much as she was loved by the public, she was loved by her sons more.

Following her death, the boys returned to school and were closeted by the family, the protocols and the traditions surrounding the House of Windsor.

William would be king one day and had to learn how to cope with the expectations of this.

It is only really now, twenty years later, that the Princes have begun to reveal their heartache, their regret at not being able to resolve their emotional crises over their mother's death.

It is a sign of how much the monarchy has changed that such honest feelings are permitted to be shared.

Diana was the catalyst for that change.

# 'One of us'

The young Diana was welcomed into the heart of the royal family as soon as it became evident that her relationship with Charles was more than just a passing fad.

'She's one of us' the Queen said of the girl, remembering the times that, as a child, Diana had played with Andrew and Edward.

Diana, for her part, did all she could to make a good impression. Playful at Balmoral, on the first proper meeting with the family, she laughed at Philip's jokes.

But underlying all of this was the anxiety she felt about mixing with her new love's closest family.

She may have caught 'the big fish' (as she later told her sister) but the river in which it swam scared her, despite her ability as a swimmer.

Doubts began to enter the Queen's mind when she saw the never ending fascination the press held for Diana.

Fearing that the girl would not cope, she organized a meeting with editors in which she requested that their coverage should be kept in hand.

Although accepted initially, before long journalists and photographers were once again cataloging her every move.

Time passed, the engagement, then wedding, happened.  To all but those most in the know, the marriage was proceeding smoothly.

By now, Diana was pregnant. William's christening fell on the birthday of the Queen Mother, and so the public's attention was spread between these two events.

What could have become an opportunity to celebrate different parts of the lives of two deeply cherished royals became a cause of consternation.

The clash seemed to cause resentment, with the young mother unhappy that attention was taken away from her son but enjoying the fact that this gave just a little more opportunity for privacy.

Matters continued apace. When Harry was born, Diana commented to a friend that she was 'not made for the production line.'

This being a reference that she wanted to be her own person, not yet another princess on the line of descent back into deepest history.

She wanted to be herself, not just another member of royalty. And she wanted her sons to have the opportunity of growing up as normally as could be achieved.

Some sympathy must be reserved for the Queen, and admiration that, since the tough times of the '80s and '90s she has led the monarchy to the more open, approachable institution that it is today.

As a young mother herself, much of the care of her children had been left to nannies, and she found it hard to understand Diana's wish to do everything for her own children.

Particularly when she had public duties to perform.

Relationships continued to be frosty, but publicly professional until the publication of Andrew Morton's serialized book, Diana.

Initially, Diana denied any involvement in the catalog of revelations. The Queen believed her, but the truth was quickly out.

The two appeared together around this time at the Trooping of the Colour, and to the public nothing could be seen to be amiss.

But at Ascot shortly afterward, Philip was seen to very obviously shun the Princess.

Diana herself feared, even more, claiming that  Palace officials had instructed the secret service to bug her home.

And, following a particularly tricky occasion when Charles wished to take his sons shooting, and Diana had them at home with her, the Prince roared down the phone to his mother.

'She's mad, mad, mad.'

But then, most marital break ups are besmirched by accusations from both sides. It's just that most break ups do not happen in the full glare of the media's interest.

The subject was put off limits by the Queen, Princess Margaret, her sister, telling friends that nobody would dare to raise it.

From the Queen's perspective, used to coping with the troubles of the nation, her training had taught her to compartmentalize issues, and so her son's crumbling marriage was to be locked away from other matters.

When the announcement finally came, made by John Major, that the Prince and Princess were to separate, the Queen was staying at Sandringham.

Her lucky corgis were treated to three successive walks, each immediately following the last, as she digested that the news was now in the public domain.

For the next few years, the country became polarized.

Diana, the young mother who put her family first, who used her celebrity to promote good causes against a royal family stuck in their ways, out of touch and bound by protocol.

At least, that is how it must have seemed to the royals.

We know now that Diana had her problems – especially with bulimia – but despite this, some occasions stand out in history.

AIDS was the plague of the time. This disease, which had seemed initially limited to the gay community, was incurable.

We began to learn that it spread through bodily fluids, hemophiliacs were particularly vulnerable until changes in procedures around blood donations led to better screening.

But the mistrust was wide amongst the public, fueled by ill-informed press coverage.

The public's attitude was not helped by the physical state of sufferers as the disease gradually destroyed them.

Pale, weak, thin – victims looked more like the recipients of crimes against humanity than sufferers of a debilitating disease.

When Diana visited a hospital, met sufferers and shook them by the hand, declaring that they needed a 'hug' rather than vilification, the public's perception began to change.

Her humanitarian outlook was genuine, not some media campaign to put her into a rose tinted light.

Right from an early age, her compassion and concern for others had been one of her most endearing traits.

On visiting Mother Theresa's hospital for the sick and dying in India, she did more than just put in an appearance to raise the profile of the good work being done.

She took the time to visit every single one of the fifty people close to death.

She was a regular visitor to the Royal Brampton Hospital in London, attending far more frequently than would be the case were it just of press coverage.

Often attending three times a week, amongst her other demanding commitments, she would spend three or four hours just talking with patients.

Towards the end of her life, she became an ardent campaigner against the use of landmines, which continued to inflect death and serious injury on innocent citizens long after war had passed.

Pictured in a field of mines in Angola, she brought the issue, largely unconsidered in the West, to everybody's attention.

As can be the way of the press, Diana's compassion and genuine kindness was presented as a direct opposite of a cold, heartless royal family.

These were just the tips of the many icebergs of her good work, which will be examined in more detail later in this biography.

Matters had seemed to reach their nadir upon publication of David Dimbleby's biography of Prince Charles, in which the Queen was presented as cold.

Her husband, Prince Philip, even worse, as a bully.

Such were the Queen's fears about the public perception of the royal family in contrast to the adulation poured on Diana, the 'victim', that she feared outcry.

She believed that the VE day 50th Anniversary celebrations would be neglected by the public but when she appeared on the balcony of Buckingham Palace, along with her sister and mother, the crowds were enormous.

That day, she appeared unemotional and stony faced. Sources close to the occasion say, though, that this was the Queen keeping her feelings under wraps.   She was close to tears.

The nation mourned Diana's death in 1997. Looking back at pictures of the bouquets, flowers and cards, it is as if a sea of the nation's tears had taken solid form.

By keeping her grandsons out of the public eye, the Queen, Prince Philip and Prince Charles protected them, but left themselves open to savage criticism.

It took many years for the public to return to the public displays of love that we see today, and during that time, there was the issue of Charles' love for Camilla to deal with.

In fact, it was Charles who was reticent, perhaps afraid of how his still young sons might react to their relationship, and certainly how the nation would.

The Queen felt that he should make his love official – after all, everybody knew about it.

His confidant, the Queen Mother felt the same.

# August, 1997

During the heat of high summer twenty years ago, Diana had flown with her boyfriend, Dodi Fayed, in his father's private jet landing at Nice in southern France.

They were due to spend time on the family's private yacht, the Jonikal.

Mohamed al Fayed, owner of Harrods, chair of Fulham FC, was a wealthy man. A very wealthy man. One who liked to get his own way.

Diana and Dodi had met at a charity event in London. Dodi, who held an established reputation as a playboy with an eye for the women, quickly struck up a friendship with the princess.

He invited her and her sons to a holiday on the yacht, which was readily accepted, photos of the boys jet skiing in the Mediterranean appearing in the tabloid press.

The boys returned to their father, leaving Dodi and Diana to make their second journey to the yacht.

Like a demented Tom and Jerry cartoon, the couple sped around the Bay of St Tropez, the press following, cramped on a small boat.

It seemed as though she was playing with them. Allowing herself to be photographed in an embrace with Fayed, diving into the sea in full view.

She even sprayed the panting paparazzi with a water pistol, promising them that a great story was about to break.

The relationship was causing angst back in the United Kingdom, Prime Minister Tony Blair warning her that the relationship was problematic.

Rumours abounded that the couple could wed. The notion of a white, Christian woman marrying a wealthy Egyptian Muslim caused ripples of consternation amongst sections of the public.

To the royal family, such a move seemed catastrophic, the future king having a Muslim step father?  Indescribable.  Such was the prevailing mood, just twenty years ago.

Diana seemed not to care. Fully and firmly held in the love of the nation, determined to be different from the expectations of royalty.

And, increasingly isolated from friends and confidants, it was as though she was testing how far she could go. How much she could get away with.

Reports from associates of the time, particularly from the al Fayed side, stated that the couple were very much in love. They seemed to be acting like love-struck teenagers.

On the one hand craving the security and support the institution of the royal family would bring, but at the same time glad to be away from its smothering embrace, Diana was understandably confused.

At the time, the security, wealth, body guards and such like that Dodi brought would be appealing to her.

But all was not well in the al Fayed dynasty; Dodi's father was very much under an unwanted spotlight.

Having failed to secure British citizenship, he had then been at the center of the cash for questions debacle that had so wounded John Major it led to the collapse of his Government.

Out of favor with the establishment, the Egyptian was keen for an alternative power base.

The House of Windsor had withdrawn their patronage of Harrods. What better way to get back than to have Diana at the heart of his new empire?

He certainly pushed his son towards the relationship. And Diana was clearly happy to go along.

On the fateful day, the penultimate day of August, 1997 Dodi and Diana had traveled to the Ritz in Paris, another piece of Mohamed al Fayed's wide ranging business.

The plan is to eat there, but the press has created chaos. Diana is so upset by the day's events, they seek to dine privately in the hotel, but the pressure is too much.

By now, excepting one short visit back to Dodi's flat, they have been in the hotel for over seven hours.

With the paparazzi crowded by the front, the couple decide to return to Dodi's apartment, but the security team are reluctant to agree.

They ask for clearance from al Fayed himself, but Dodi persuades them that they could leave by a back entrance, and will escape unnoticed.

The plan involves leaving his chauffeur at the hotel, whilst head of security, Henri Paul, drives them home.

In the car with Paul, sits Trevor Rees, Dodi's bodyguard, the only person who will survive the crash.

Dodi and Diana are in the back of the Mercedes.

Actual events are, to this day, unclear. The Mercedes leaves the Ritz, but the paparazzi are not fooled.

Chasing the story, anxious for anything that might sell, they follow the car.

A motorcycle pulls up alongside the limo at a set of traffic lights, camera flashing. Paul loses him as they pull away from the lights, pushing the Mercedes to speeds of 70MPH.

The car is a big beast, and later it emerges that it has seen some tough times, been involved in smashes that might have finished other cars.

It is also the case that Paul has been drinking, with tests showing him to be three times over the legal limit, the alcohol mixing with anti depressant drugs.

They reach the Pont de l'Alma tunnel with the Mercedes hurtling at break neck speeds. The tunnel dips and turns making it tricky enough to navigate for any large vehicle.

Impossible for one speeding.

The most probable chain of events sees it catch up with a white Fiat, clipping it and crashing into the concrete Pillar 13 of the tunnel.

It is all over. The Fiat is never discovered.

An off duty doctor arrives within thirty seconds. Clarity is even further lost from this point on. Stories conflict, drifting in and out of public favor.

Everyone loves a conspiracy, everyone loves a mystery. Being there makes you hot property and your story is worth a bob or two.

Extracting truth from fabrication becomes impossible.

Rees, the bodyguard, claims that Diana was calling for Dodi.

The Doctor insists that she was unconscious, with no obvious signs of external injury.

The paparazzi descend, cameras flashing as they photograph the car's dead and dying inhabitants.

Several are later arrested for causing the crash, but all are eventually found not guilty. The evidence is that they had not been there when the crash happened.

The extent to which their presence caused the alcohol influenced Paul to drive so dangerously is harder to judge.

The fire brigade releases the passengers, cutting open the mangled vehicle. Prior to this, emergency workers try to treat the injured Princess.

By now, she is conscious, thrashing about and refusing treatment, incoherent and clearly hurt. The approach of death is meritocratic, it scares us all.

She had not been wearing her seatbelt, and her injuries are consistent with her having been half turned when the collision occurred.

Looking for the chasing paparazzi? Playing a game? Who knows?

By 1.30 in the morning of August 31st, just over an hour after the crash, Diana is taken by ambulance to hospital. She has, by this time, already suffered one cardiac arrest.

Dodi is pronounced dead at the scene.

As the ambulance speeds towards the hospital, Diana's condition deteriorates further. The vehicle stops to administer adrenaline before arriving at the hospital at just past two a.m.

At the hospital, open heart massage is performed for two hours, but her injuries are too severe.

At 4.00 a.m. Diana is pronounced dead.

Back home, her sons are asleep at Balmoral Castle.

# Finding The Truth

From almost the moment that it is announced that Diana has been killed, stories, lies, conspiracies and rumor combine to blur the truth.

Stories circulate that Diana walked away from the crash site, only to die later. Allegations that the French hospital did not attempt to save her life are poured out.

Such dreadful insinuations are allowed, for a time, to remain in the public eye.

Dodi el Fayed's life is analyzed in even greater detail. Was he really the fun loving, womanizing playboy that he is made out to be, or is he more complicated?

Another theory is that Dodi was much more insecure. Despite his father's attempts to get the facts covered up, he had never really made a success of his various ventures.

Whilst at Sandhurst he regularly over spent on his £400000 per month allowance.

He was at the Officer training camp in Berkshire undertaking a short course in leadership, something popular with the sons of wealthy men from the Middle East at the time.

Various girlfriends came forward to tell their stories – that he was more anxious to be seen with a beautiful girl than commit to her.

His film producing career fell flat. In fact, what emerged was a rather sad picture of a man who was frighteningly wealthy, but in awe of his father.

He sought approval from his father in all that he did. Stories quickly circulated that maybe his relationship with Diana was far less serious than thought.

Perhaps it was something pushed by his father as a way of getting back at the royal family who, Mohamed al Fayed felt, had snubbed him because of his Egyptian background.

Certainly, the Harrods' owner pushed his own theories surrounding his son's death – murder, as he called it - using all the power that his billions could employ.

He built a shrine to Dodi inside Harrods. He sought to blame the royal family for his son's death, arguing that they had ordered MI6 to assassinate the couple.

He also blamed his own bodyguards for their incompetence (both leave his employment). He then shifts blame to Prince Philip.

Another twist occurs when an eye witness claims to have seen a massive flash of white just before the crash.

A former spy asks to speak to the inquest, and states that the British Secret Service had hatched a plan to kill the Serbian leader Slobodan Milosevic.

This involved blinding a driver with a bright flash, and was planned to happen in a tunnel.

Almost a carbon copy of what some had claimed happened in the Paris underpass.

Various allegations are made regarding the white Fiat. One witness states that they were nearly hit by such a vehicle as it left the tunnel, swerving wildly with the driver looking backwards.

Police hear reports that a large dog was in the back. They claim to have found the vehicle, but then dismiss it as not being the one.

Mohamed al Fayed says that his investigators have discovered the car, and that it belongs to a member of the paparazzi, but that particular story dies a death.

French judges, Herve Stephan and Marie-Christine Devidal are appointed to lead an investigation into the event.

The Royal Coronor, John Burton, will hold an inquest in Britain later.

It takes over two years for the French judge's report to be published. It lays the blame squarely on the shoulders of Paul, stating that he was driving over the limit.

He also had prescription drugs in his system and was driving at speeds that were far too high. The paparazzi charged at the time of the deaths have all accusations dropped.

Mohamed al Fayed is furious at these conclusions and unsuccessfully petitions the French courts to review their findings.

He is also unsuccessful in his wish for a joint inquest to be held into the deaths of his son and Diana.

By the time that an official announcement takes place that there will be a British inquest, John Burton has left his post, and been replaced by another coroner, Michael Burgess.

Shortly after this, al Fayed once again hits the headlines when he announces that Diana had telephoned him on the night she died, to tell him that she was pregnant, and the baby was his son's.

Over six years after the accident, the British inquest finally gets underway, and a day later an inquiry into Diana's death is announced.

But seven months in, Burgess resigns, and is replaced by Dame Elizabeth Butler-Sloss. Months later, she too is replaced, Lord Justice Scott Baker taking control of the inquest.

It begins again in October 2007, over ten years after the crash. Six months later, it reports.

The verdict is that both Diana and Dodi were unlawfully killed.

It is hard to conclude that the process was anything other than a complete mess. In the mean time, the princes had moved through their teenage years and into adulthood without their mother.

From the moment that they had learned of their mother's death, early one morning in

Scotland, they had been protected as far as possible.

At their own request, they had attended church that morning, then moved into the protective curtain of the royal family.

The world had been touched at their appearance at Diana's funeral but then they had returned to their schools, the press perhaps learning their lesson and largely keeping away from them.

The royal family too had learned. The enormous outpouring of national grief that followed Diana's death taught them that they had to be more open to the public.

Of course, the family is made up of separate individuals who deserve their privacy. But it is also a national institution – a Commonwealth institution.

Royals are born into privilege – a life of service but also a life of wealth and access to things about which the rest of us can only dream.

They had learned that this comes with a price.

From her funeral at Westminster Abbey, Diana was taken to her family home in Northamptonshire.

The journey was by road, with the pavements lined with mourners.

In Northampton, the nearest town to Althorp, special measures were put in place to deal with the influx. Hospital beds were freed up, and mental health facilities were on special alert.

Nobody was really sure how some elements of the public might react to the tragedy, risks needed to be anticipated.

But all went well, and Diana was interred on a small island in the grounds of the Althorp estate, in a private ceremony, away from the eyes of all but her closest family.

# Close Relationships

Another man featured in Diana's life, heavily
so, he would like us to believe. This was
Paul Burrell, her butler and, possibly, her
confidant through many of her most
troubled times.

Burrell claims that he was, to Diana, the one
man she could trust. Diana's self proclaimed
rock had been a footman in Buckingham
Palace before becoming butler to Charles and
Di.

Amongst his stories is one where she
claimed that she was being followed and
feared for her life, and he also says that she
wrote him a note predicting her death in a
road accident.

His many revelations have had an impact on his life since Diana's death. He wrote two books, to help look after his family, he says.

However, his actions have seen him sidelined by the royals. William and Harry have not spoken to him since their mother's death, and Prince Charles does not stay in touch.

Even Diana's family have been cold towards the man who confesses that he said too much about her relationships and problems.

However, he says that he still sees the Queen from time to time – 'she listens well,' he explains.

He also offers insight into Diana's relationship with another man.

Diana and Hasnet Khan had a close and loving relationship, according to the former butler. Hasnat was the true love of her life.

Dr Khan, a cardiologist, had a two year affair with Diana, and it ended in 1997, just before her death. She called him Mr Wonderful.

Burrell claims that he was the fixer between the two, acting as a go between and purchasing gifts for the doctor from the Princess.

Diana's relationship with her mother, Frances, was another into which Burrell expressed public opinions.

Although the two had remained emotionally close after her mother left and her father gained custody of the Diana and her siblings, there are claims of a breakdown close to her death.

Apparently, Frances Shane Kydd – as she was known by this point – disapproved of the religious background of Hasnet Khan, a Muslim.

During a phone call between mother and daughter, to which Burrell said Diana asked him to listen, Kydd poured drunken criticism down the phone.

This was aimed at, in particular, Hasnet and another friend of the Princess, Gulu Lalvani.

Unable to take any more, Diana hung up and sobbed, sitting on the carpet of the sitting room.

Burrell has also claimed that tensions ran high within the Spencer household, especially after the death of Diana's father, Johnnie.

He said that her sister was struck by jealousy and her brother, the current Earl, had instigated her burial on the island at Althorp, describing it as 'lonely and isolated.'

Diana's affair with James Hewitt had involved them spending weekends at the officer's Devon getaway – a cottage belonging to his mother.

When the extra marital relationship ended in 1991 Hewitt was devastated.

Diana's former bodyguard met with him over dinner to tell him that affair could not be resurrected. But like Khan and al Fayed, stories about Hewitt have remained bubbling under in the media world.

News rises from time to time, before returning him once more to a footnote in the life of the People's Princess.

His current poor state of health has once again put him into the headlines, especially with the twentieth anniversary of Diana's death much in the news.

# The People's Princess

'The kindness and affection from the public have carried me through some of the most difficult periods, and always your love and affection have eased the journey,' said Princess Diana to the adoring population.

One of the things that endeared her to the population at large was her openness. This was for many reasons.

It satisfied the public's desire for gossip and knowledge about the previously secret royal family; it provided a counterpoint to the closed shop of the rest of the family.

But perhaps more than this, it made people realize that if somebody as iconic as Diana could talk about her depression, her loves,

her bulimia and her dark times, then so
could they.

She was 'one of us' whilst retaining an aura
of specialness that kept her apart, and added
a mystery to her that sustained public
interest.

Another reason for such popularity was her
kindness. Not only in her support of
charities, of Aids victims and suchlike,
although there was much of that, but in her
everyday life.

She was simply a lovely person. It is hard to
find, beyond perhaps some contemporary
outpourings from the Palace, anybody with a
bad word for her.

She had a ready smile for everybody, that – despite her deep shyness – she would talk to anybody.

These are the stories that count, more than affairs with millionaire playboys or rows with heirs to the throne.

Her mischievous nature can be illustrated by an event that happened in the late 1980s. She had spent the evening with a group of friends, including Queen's Freddy Mercury and comedian Kenny Everett.

On discovering that they planned to go on to a notorious gay bar in London, the Vauxhall Tavern, she insisted on joining them.

She wanted to sneak in unknown to the media, and just have a night of fun. A rummage around the flat took place, and five minutes later they had found the perfect disguise.

Dressed like an extra from 'Top Gun' the Princess successfully navigated into the bar, and had – according to friends – a terrific time.

Many people have simple tales of her kindness. A teacher at a school against which her sons played when at Ludgrove recalls how interested she was in the lives of the staff.

How she would remember stories and ask again how things were going even though it might be six months, even a year, since they had last met. All this at a time when her own life was undergoing enormous turmoil.

The American writer, Bill Bryson, reports an incident when he is aimlessly wandering along a track in Windsor Great Park.

Aware that he is holding up a vehicle, and could have been for some time, he moves aside, expecting a mouthful of abuse.

Instead, he receives the most wonderful, warm smile from the driver of the vehicle, who is, of course, Diana.

Women, in particular, found ways of echoing her through the clothes they wore. As a trendsetter in fashion, her styles were copied in High Street stores.

The press and fashion industry were always ready for her newest look. Diana herself tended to favor the big name labels, but she created a style that was easily, and readily, copied.

Her face was everywhere. She appeared on the cover of People Magazine no fewer than fifty times, and was the photo on the front page of Time and Newsweek on numerous occasions as well.

Her portraits seem omnipresent; photographs on club walls, paintings in military messes, official and commissioned art in major galleries.

Her commitment to charities was absolute, she was patron to over one hundred – many of her duties passed on to her sons.

Much has been spoken about her work with Aids sufferers and the plague of landmines, but some of the lesser publicized good works she supported deserve attention.

It is hard to imagine a group in more direct contrast to the royal family in Britain than homeless teenagers.

Not least thanks to Diana's work the problem is now less prevalent. Walking on the South Bank in London in the 1990s many would have passed the cardboard city.

This haunt of the homeless was just yards from the Thames, close to some of the wealthiest parts of the world. But in those days, it was just a ghetto of cardboard and poverty.

Diana was a driving force behind Centrepoint, a charity that seeks to support and take homeless teenagers forwards in their lives.

Prince William is an avid campaigner for the organization today.

Not many people know much about leprosy beyond bible studies from school. But the disfiguring and deadly disease remains a scourge in parts of the world.

Her work with the Leprosy Mission helped thousands of children suffering from the terrible infliction.

Her love and support for children was legendary. Indeed, it was her attitude to her own two that brought one of the sharpest contrasts with the traditions of the monarchy.

She supported both Great Ormand Street Hospital, which is specifically for children, and the cancer hospital, the Royal Marsden. Here, she would often be seen talking to and hugging young victims.

Although she did support some charities that represented activities close to her heart, the English National Ballet for example, the overwhelming majority were humanitarian causes.

# A Wonderful Legacy

Undoubtedly, one of the greatest legacies of Diana is the work her children now do.

Look through official or, particularly, unplanned snaps and the reciprocated warmth that comes through to the boys is so obvious.

William has recently revealed how sad he is that his own children will never know their grandmother, and that her wisdom and influence can only be passed on second hand.

His younger brother talks about the enormous hole that was blown into his life, and that it was only recently, when he entered his late twenties, that he was able to begin the process of coming to terms with it.

But, despite the tragedy and heartache, the loss and void that filled their lives, they have taken forward much of her charitable work.

Each takes a prominent position in charities supporting the poor in Africa. Prince Harry, who spent some of his gap year working with AIDS sufferers, runs the charity Sentebale.

This specifically looks to support the poorest children in Botswana and Lesotho, helping AIDS and HIV victims in particular.

He works with Prince Seeiso of Lesotho and both share the memory of mothers who worked tirelessly for Aids victims.

Like his mother, Harry has a particular drive for charities related to the continent. Diana's passion to eradicate land mines led to several countries signing up to an agreement to ban them.

Harry continues to promote her message, urging the world to be free of the weapons by 2025.

William maintains the work of his mother in supporting endangered species on the continent. He is patron of Tusk Trust.

Harry's drive to improve understanding of AIDS and its impact is unrelenting.

He has worked for the Terence Higgins Trust, and was recently shown live on Facebook undertaking an AIDS test to help remove the stigma surrounding the process.

This followed him joining with the singer Rihanna to undergo public HIV testing in Barbados.

The Princes continue to promote their mother's work with children - Harry is patron of Wellchild. This important charity seeks to support seriously ill children to get out of hospital and back to their families.

A range of wide spread and previously unspeakable disease which affects millions of adults and children in Britain relate to mental health.

By speaking openly about her own self harming and mental health illness, Diana brought this issue, for so long hidden behind euphemism and silence, more into the open.

During her well known 1995 interview with journalist Martin Bashir she revealed how there could be days that she was so low, she simply did not want to leave her bed.

As with her African charities, and AIDS/HIV support, her sons have taken this matter under their wings. Prince William and his wife, Kate Middleton, along with Harry, recently opened the Heads Together programme.

This seeks to bring into the open mental health concerns by encouraging discussion about the subject. During interviews, Harry was prepared to talk about his own mental health problems.

It is another of Diana's legacies that she helped to create the environment where a royal felt able to talk about such issues.

It is hard to imagine this happening twenty or thirty years ago, when such a concern might be swept under the carpet with the brush of 'Get on with it.'

Harry's concerns related to his grieving process for his mother.

Both princes have used their own experience of loss and grief to help others. William is a patron of Child Bereavement UK. He works with and supports children who have lost their parents.

On an individual level, to be counseled, supported and recognized by people of such high profile as the princes, or before them, their mother, must help those in pain.

But alongside this, it is the very profile that these people hold that brings their cause to wider attention, helping others directly through matters such as fundraising.

But also through simply raising understanding and reducing stigma for the young, ill and vulnerable people who suffer now, or might in the future.

It is a fine legacy to leave.


In the build up to the twentieth anniversary of her death, William and Harry announced plans to erect a statue in her memory.

This will be in the public gardens around Kensington Palace, and the scheme has the approval of the Queen. A floral tribute is also planned.

Her role as a fashion icon has been remembered with a special exhibition in Kensington Palace that charts her changing styles over the 80s and 90s.

The Diana Award is another way in which her legacy is being maintained. This is awarded to young people who create and sustain positive social change through their actions.

At a time of great division within our, and other, societies, anything that helps to bring young people together for good would undoubtedly earn her absolute approval.

If only she were alive to grant it.

Millennials have grown up with only second hand reports of Diana Spencer's acts. Her incredible kindness, humanitarianism as well as her flaws exist outside of their lifetimes.

But she remains in the thoughts of the public.

It is her flaws that, in many ways, endear her to the population. During a time in which the House of Windsor sought to hide the inevitable tensions and problems any family endures, she was spoke her truths.

By sharing her worries, her mental illness, her problems she brought them into our lives, and helped to demystify them.

And, she made herself more like us.

Perfect Princesses only exist in fairy tales and Disney Films, but Princess Diana showed

that it was possible to have access to
incredible wealth, opportunity and privilege.

But also to be human, with the flaws and
compromises this entails.

This is why she became the People's
Princess.

# Conclusion - An Impossible Story

Imagine for a moment that you were charged with creating a story. A tragedy. How would you proceed?

You may well choose a tale in which a sweet, beautiful girl grows up; a lovely kind girl, who might even have an infatuation with a famous man...maybe even a prince.

You might concoct the situation where she could meet this Prince and be swept off her feet. Your plot twist would need to come soon, a third character should be introduced.

Not a wicked stepmother, that's already been done, but a presence that disturbs the equalibrium.

Your subplot might even involve this character coming good in the end.

You would want to make your heroine a wonderful person, whose acts warm the hearts of those around her. She would need an inner strength to give her depth and character.

She would need to stand up for her independence, protect her children and overcome the breakdown of her first love.

And like all heroes and heroines, she would need a flaw. But despite this flaw, she would be loved by everybody, an icon to lift the mood of the world.

She would need to come to a tragic end, an accident cutting her down when she appeared to have finally found love once more.

At this point, the cynical might suggest that you are taking the story too far, taking liberties with artistic license.

That you are reaching a point beyond improbability.

But you would continue, your heroine's legacy established, personified through her children who replace her in the affections of the world.

But, no. Stories like that don't really happen. Do they?